BACKSLIDING
IN HEART

Contents

Contents

SLIPPING AWAY FROM GOD

WHEN WE BELIEVERS backslide, we often backslide slowly, and quietly. In fact, most times we backslide so slowly and so quietly that we don't even realize that we are backsliding. Our backsliding doesn't usually begin with some loud, shocking act of sin – such as going out and buying and using illegal drugs, getting drunk and making a scene, or committing fornication. *No...backsliding usually begins when we allow our relationship with the Lord to deteriorate.*

When we slip away from our relationship with God, our hearts begin to slide away from Him. Everything that follows is a result of the loss of a thriving, intimate relationship with God.

Turn with me to Matthew 26, where Peter's life shows us the steps to a backsliding heart ... and back again.

You Will All Fall Away

Matthew 26 brings us to the legendary scene of the Last Supper. The twelve disciples had gathered together around the table to share a Passover meal with Jesus. This was one of the most special occasions of the year for this small group of first-century Jews. The disciples were no doubt hoping to hear Jesus share some words of encouragement.

Jesus was aware that this was to be the last occasion on which they would all be together before His death on the cross and resurrection soon after. The words He was to speak would be etched in history for all the ages to come. These words would very likely echo in the hearts of His disciples till their last days on earth. Jesus could have used this special occasion to say all kinds of encouraging things to His disciples, and I am sure that is what the disciples were hoping for.

Perhaps the disciples hoped to hear something like this:

"You guys are amazing in every way! I love your passion for Me! I love your dedication to Me and My words! I love the way you love one another and have stayed focused day after day as we traveled together! You have stuck with Me this entire time, and we've seen great things happen wherever we have gone. Thank you, thank you, thank you."

But that isn't what Jesus chose to say. In fact, what He chose to say wasn't encouraging at all. He told the disciples something that would have sent a wave of shock through the room:

"This very night, you will all fall away on account of Me."

The words rang in the disciples' ears. "We will all fall away on account of you?"

The disciples knew immediately what Jesus meant. The word translated "fall away" in English is the Greek word *skandalizo*, from which we get the English word scandal. The word *skandalizo* carries a simple meaning in Greek: "to be offended." In other words, Jesus was telling His disciples this:

"This very night, every single one of you is going to be offended because of Me. My name, and your position as My disciples, are going to become a scandal to you."

Each of the disciples probably reacted to Jesus' words in his own way. Each of the disciples, like us, had a unique role, personality, and set of strengths and weaknesses. Peter's reaction to Jesus' words is the case that is most clearly explained in the book of Matthew. In order to understand Peter's reaction, let's take a look into his personality.

Peter's Personality

What was Peter like? In the Bible we see that among the disciples Peter was an energetic leader with a Type A personality. He was the kind of disciple who would have often said things such as: "Come on, guys! Anyone want to go witness?" "Let's go heal someone!" or "Anybody want to pray?" He was the masculine leader—an alpha male—who had the ability to rally everyone up for Jesus, saying, "We can do this!" But I believe that in his heart of hearts, Peter thought that he was more spiritual than all the other disciples. He thought he was more faithful to Jesus than they were. This attitude of his heart is revealed in how he replies to Jesus' words, "This very night, you will all fall away on account of me."

Not Me, Lord!

Peter replied, "Even if all fall away on account of you, I never will." (Matthew 26:23)

Do see the state of heart Peter was in? He was essentially saying, "Not me, Lord! I will still be standing! The other disciples might all fall away, but I won't!" Peter's remarks reveal the poor state of his heart. Indeed, Peter had *already* begun to fall away from the Lord.

How do I know? Because Peter was in sin. Peter had been caught in broad daylight with a heart full of one of the sneakiest, most damaging sins in existence: "spiritual pride."

Has your heart ever been "spiritually prideful"? Mine has, and I can tell you that it is a miserable condition to be in. When we become convinced that we are more spiritual than everyone else, it is usually because our hearts are filled with false judgments towards others. This state of heart is so displeasing to our Father and so damaging to those around us! God wants us to give others the benefit of the doubt and to "consider others as more valuable than ourselves" (Philippians 2:3). When we are full of false judgment, we may have the external appearance of spirituality, but we can be sure that on the inside we are starting to fall away from the Lord. This was certainly the case for Peter, and Jesus made no "buts" about it.

Jesus' Shocking Reply

Jesus' next words would have come as a shock to Peter:

"Truly I tell you, this very night, before the rooster crows, you will disown (deny) me three times." (Matthew 26:24)

But Peter, insistent that He would never fall away, refused to question his own faithfulness to Jesus. He declared, "Even if I have to die with you, I will never disown you."

Peter not only *claimed* that He would never disown Jesus but he *declared* that he would never disown Him. In doing so, he pulled the other disciples into the same deception, as we see in the next verse: "And all the other disciples said the same."

How About Us?

Now before we think too poorly of Peter, let's consider our own lives. Let's be honest. If we had been in Peter's position, and Jesus had told *us* that we would deny Him, many of us would have been shocked to hear it as well. In our hearts, some of us would have probably felt the same way Peter felt.... "That's not going to happen. Not me, Lord! No way." Why? Because some of us are blinded by an infection of spiritual pride, too! We have been blinded by our pride in the same way we could be blinded by some form of blatant outward sin.

I hate to be able to admit this, but there have been times when I have been stuck in both spiritual pride *and* blatant outward sin, even as a believer. Have you ever had a time like that? Are you in a time like that now? 1 Thessalonians 5:19 tells us "Do not quench the Spirit." In those times, the flow of the Holy Spirit is blocked in our lives. We quench the Holy Spirit, and it is impossible to sense the presence of the Lord in the way that we do when we walk closely and humbly with our God.

That is just where Peter was, but Jesus stayed with him and asked him for his help as long as he was willing to give it.

PART 1: BACKSLIDING

STEP 1: RELATIONAL DENIAL

Step #1 of a Backsliding Heart – Relational Denial

After the Passover meal Jesus went with the disciples to the Garden of Gethsemane, knowing that the hour of His crucifixion was approaching. Let's take a moment to read the biblical account of what happened in Matthew 26:36-39 (NIV).

"Jesus went with his disciples to a place called Gethsemane and he said to them, 'Sit here while I go over there and pray.' He took Peter and the two sons of Zebedee along with him, and he began to be sorrowful and troubled. Then He said to them, 'My soul is overwhelmed with sorrow to the point of death. Stay here and keep watch with me.' Going a little further, he fell with his face to the ground and prayed, 'My Father, if it is possible, may this cup be taken from me. Yet not as I will, but as you will.'"

After Jesus prayed, He came out of the garden and found a pack of sleeping disciples and asked Peter:

"Couldn't you men keep watch with me for a single hour?" (Matthew 26:40)

Remember that only a few hours earlier Peter had *declared* his unfading faithfulness to Jesus.

"Watch and pray so that you will not fall into temptation. The Spirit is willing but the flesh is weak. He went away a second time and prayed, 'My Father, if it is not possible for this cup to be taken away unless I drink it, may your will be done.' When He came back, He again found them sleeping, because their eyes were heavy. So He left them and went away once more and prayed a third time, saying the same thing. Then He returned to the disciples and said to them, 'Are you still sleeping and resting.'" (Matthew 26:41-45)

The Greek word used for *keep watch* is *gregorio,* which means "to be watchful, to be awake, to be vigilant." All Jesus had asked Peter and the other disciples to do was to be watchful, awake, and vigilant for a single hour! But when Jesus came back He found that they had all fallen asleep. This is an example of what I call "relational denial," or the neglect of an intimate relationship with the Lord. They did it three times in a row during Jesus' call to prayer. How about that?

All the disciples had denied Jesus relationally by denying Him the prayer support He had asked for. But instead of directing the probing question to all of the disciples, Jesus directed it specifically to Peter, the disciple who had solemnly declared, "Even if all fall away on account of you, I never will."

Jesus emphasized the relational denial of Peter more than the others because Peter thought He was a more faithful disciple than the others.

How About Us?

Just as in Peter's case, the first step to a backsliding heart is when we deny Jesus in our personal relationship with Him. God is depending on us to stay in communication with Him, to listen to Him, and to talk to Him. Are we falling asleep?

Are you denying Jesus in your relationship with Him? In the Garden of Gethsemane, Jesus was depending on the disciples to pray for Him, but they got distracted and fell asleep. Likewise, there are a million ways that we can get distracted from our relationship with God, lulling us into spiritual slumber. Are we falling asleep? Are *you* falling asleep?

If you are being drawn away from your relationship with the Lord, think of what is keeping you from pursuing Him. Hebrews 12:1 says, "Therefore, since we are surrounded by such a great cloud of witnesses, let us throw off everything that hinders and the sin that so easily entangles. And let us run with perseverance the race marked out for us." God is saying through His word: "If something is slowing you down, cast it off!"

STEP 2: FOLLOWING AT A DISTANCE

STEP #2 – Following Jesus at a Distance

"Those who had arrested Jesus took him to Caiaphas the high priest, where the teachers of the law and the elders had assembled. But Peter followed him at a distance." *(Matthew 26:57-58)*

When you are spending time with someone you love, don't you like to walk close to him or her? Similarly, if you are somewhat ashamed of someone, you might not want to walk too close to him. When I was a teenager, before I became a Christian, I worked hard at trying to be "cool" and so at times I didn't want to be seen walking with my parents. I would try to follow them at a distance, as though I was walking by myself. This is the same as in Peter's case: After his relational denial in the garden, he began to follow Jesus at a distance.

A wonderful quote I heard many years ago relates to the backslider's situation, because backsliding starts with a thought and how we react to that thought.

> *"If you sow a thought, you reap an act.*
>   *If you sow an act, you reap a habit.*
>   *If you sow a habit, you reap a lifestyle.*
>   *If you sow a lifestyle, you reap your destiny."*

So what happened with Peter? Because of Peter's relational denial of Jesus in the garden, he began to feel comfortable with following Jesus at a distance. This shows us an important principle: If we have been denying Jesus relationally, and denying our Father the quality private time that He wants and deserves from us, we will surely begin to follow Jesus at a distance. This plays out, for instance, when we have an opportunity to say something about Jesus in public, and instead of showing commitment to Him, we show embarrassment and keep silent.

Matthew 26:28 gives us even more insight into Peter's situation:

> *"Peter followed him at a distance, right up to the courtyard of the high priest. He entered and sat down with the guards to see the outcome."*

Peter didn't just follow Jesus at a distance and stand off to the side. He entered into the place where the guards were and sat down with them. He sat down with the people that were against Jesus, like he was part of them. This was a dangerous step backwards. "What fellowship does light have with darkness?"

What About Us?

Instead of looking down on Peter for his compromise, let's take a journey into our own hearts. Let's take a moment to honestly ask ourselves, "Where am I today?" Each and every one of us is currently at one of the five points on the road of backsliding and restoration that we are describing in this book.

Some Honest Questions for All of Us

We *all need* to ask ourselves some honest questions. If you are reading this booklet, please take a moment to really think of the true answers to these questions. Please take some time and write out your answers to the following questions.

❶ Am I sitting down with the world?

_____

_____

_____

❷ Am I getting comfortable with the things of the world?

_____

_____

_____

❸ Is my heart becoming conformed to this world or to the image of Christ?

_____

_____

_____

❹ Am I watching the same things that the world watches?

_____

_____

❺ Am I listening to the same things the world is listening to?

_____

_____

❻ Am I speaking some of the same words that the world speaks?

_____

_____

❼ If so, is it because I don't want to be offensive or politically incorrect?

_____

_____

❽ By my life, do I make it seem as if Jesus didn't mean the things He said?

_____

_____

_____

If so, this whole time *we are denying Him*!

STEP 3: PUBLIC DENIAL

Step #3 – Public Denial (Disownment)

At this point in the book, you are probably pretty shocked at Peter's heart condition – and maybe even at your own. But Peter's road away from God hasn't ended yet. First, he relationally denied Jesus in the garden, when he slept instead of praying three times. Then he followed Jesus at a distance, and even sat down with Jesus' enemies. But now, he was about to do something worse than he had ever imagined possible … he was about to publicly deny, to disown Jesus entirely.

Peter's Denial

While Peter was sitting in the courtyard with the enemies of Jesus, a servant girl saw him, and recognized him. She said:

"You also were with Jesus of Galilee." (Matthew 26:69)

Here the servant girl accused Peter of being a disciple of Jesus. He was, of course, and this was the perfect opportunity for him to change his course and confess Jesus as he had *declared* he would even if he had to die for it! But Peter did not choose to confess his relationship with Jesus. Instead, he chose to deny that he was a disciple of Jesus.

> *"He denied it before them all. 'I don't know what you're talking about,' he said." (Matthew 26:70)*

Peter's Disownment

In fear, Peter walked out to the gateway, away from those he had been sitting with. He hoped to walk to a place where no one would point out that he was Jesus' disciple. But just the opposite happened. Another servant girl recognized him and told all those around her:

> *"This fellow was with Jesus of Nazareth." (Matthew 26:71)*

In a rush of fear and anger, Peter did something that he never thought he would do:

> *"He denied it again, with an oath: 'I don't know the man!'" (Matthew 26:72)*

The first time Peter denied Jesus, he said, "I don't know what you are talking about." But now he took it a huge step further. He not only denied his identity as a disciple of Jesus but denied and disowned Jesus, and that with an oath, saying, "I don't know the man!"

I am sure that when Peter spoke these words something inside of him began to ache. He *did* know Jesus. He had known Jesus in *such* an intimate, personal, and powerful way. But this spiritual cancer called pride had invaded his heart, and it was changing him.

After all Peter had said to deny Jesus, the people still didn't believe his words. So Peter went even further in his denial and disownment of the Lord Jesus. So far, each time he denied Jesus, he did it with increased feeling. Now he was about to deny Jesus louder than ever.

Calling Down Curses

> *"After a little while, those standing there went up to Peter and said, 'Surely you are one of them; your accent gives you away.' Then he began to call down curses, and he swore to them, 'I don't know the man!'" (Matthew 26:73-74)*

Jesus says in Matthew 12:37 (KJV), "For by thy words thou shalt be justified, and by thy words thou shalt be condemned." The Bible also says in Proverbs 18:21 that "life and death are in the power of the tongue." What Peter did was a very powerful thing! Peter not only publicly denied Jesus but literally called down curses on himself.

The word here for "curse" is the word *katanathematizo*. When you break this word down in the Greek, you find that is a compound of two words. The first word is the word *kata* which quite often denotes intensity. It intensifies the word that follows it. The other word is the word *anathematizo*, which means to bind under a curse, bind with an oath, or bind under a great curse. When you put the two words together you have the strongest verbal denial possible. This was not a good choice on Peter's part! Everyone who heard his words that night knew he had just used the strongest rejection word in his vocabulary to deny Jesus.

It was then that Peter realized how far he had fallen. Possibly in that moment he remembered how Jesus had called him when he was a foul-mouthed fisherman and made him into a disciple of the Son of God. It was then that Peter saw clearly what he had done, and that brought him to the next step: *Repentance.*

Leonard Ravenhill once said:

"There are three people living inside of us: The one we think we are, the one others think we are and the one God knows we are."

Because God loved Peter so much, He allowed certain things to happen to bring Peter to a place where he would see the true state of his heart and lose his prideful confidence in himself. Only *then* would he come to be truly dependent upon the Lord.

Sometimes that is the only way that we seem to understand our frailty. If you've backslidden in heart, won't you do this now:

"Consider how far you have fallen, repent and do the things you did at first." (Revelation 2:5 NIV)

PART 2: AND BACK AGAIN

STEP 4: REPENTANCE

Step #4 – Repentance

Step number four is where things begin to change for the better. Let's look at what takes place in this story.

> "*Immediately a rooster crowed. Then Peter remembered the word Jesus had spoken: 'Before the rooster crows, you will disown me three times.' And he went outside and wept bitterly.*" (Matthew 26:74-75)

Earlier, when Jesus spoke to them and bore his heart in the garden, he said, "My soul is overwhelmed with sorrow to the point of death." I believe that Peter had a similar feeling in this moment. He was overwhelmed with sorrow for what he had done and could not believe that he had actually done it.

That is true repentance. Repentance isn't merely being sorry for being caught in sin. True repentance is being sorrowful over the sin, seeing the state of heart that brought you to the place where you could commit the sin, and turning away from that state of heart totally and completely.

God will always give grace to those who are truly humbled by their sin. James 4:6 says: "God opposes the proud but gives grace to the humble." If we have backslidden in heart, then we need to come to Him and say, "Lord, have mercy on me, a sinner." Something happens in the heart of God when we come to Him with a broken and contrite spirit. In the midst of brokenness, God hears our prayer and opens wide the throne of His grace.

God's Formula for Revival

And what is God's response to man's repentance? Acts 3:19 tells us:

> *"Repent and return, so that your sins may be wiped away, in order that times of refreshing may come from the presence of the Lord."*

What happens when we repent is that God brings us to a place of restoration, which brings us to a place of renewal, which then brings us into revival.

You see, I am not waiting for revival to "hit" and awaken people and churches all over the city out of spiritual slumber. I am not going to sit around doing nothing, just waiting passively for revival to come. I believe God is calling us to *walk in revival!* God is calling us to repent of our sins and turn to Him, that the times of refreshing may come from the presence of the Lord. There is no use praying for times of revival until we repent and return to God. If we see that we have a backsliding heart, it's time to turn away from the sins that are crippling us and turn towards

Jesus, the Savior. God will restore us, but not until we repent! Once we have returned to God, we will be ready to carry Jesus' message to others in the power of the Holy Spirit.

Empowered to Carry Revival

Do you have the Holy Spirit? If you will begin to walk in the power and purity of the Holy Spirit, you will see things that accompany revival. Revival is simply stepping back into what God had planned for His people all along. He modeled it in the book of Acts. Revival is just a return to normal New Testament Christianity.

If we are walking in revival, we will follow God's commands. We will step out in faith and pray for people and preach the Gospel. We will pray for the sick, and they, believing, will be healed. We will pray and preach according to the promises of God, not according to our experience, which can be great or limited, full of successes or failures. God is calling us to take the opportunities He provides for us to walk in the power of the Holy Spirit every day! Once we have turned from our sins back to Jesus, we will live the exciting life that God calls us to.

So, friend, what is holding you back from Jesus? Take a while to pray and think it over. And decide now to turn from it and turn back to Him.

STEP 5: RESTORATION

Step #5 – Restoration

Earlier, at the Passover table, Jesus had promised Peter: "before the rooster crows, you will deny me three times." That prophecy came to pass, to Peter's shame. But now Jesus was giving Peter three opportunities to verbally reaffirm his faith in Jesus, his commitment to Jesus, and his love for Jesus. In this process, Jesus is restoring him into relationship and into ministry.

> *"So when they had eaten breakfast, Jesus said to Simon Peter, 'Simon, son of John, do you love Me more than these?' He said to Him, 'Yes, Lord; You know that I love You.' He said to him, 'Feed My lambs.'" (John 21:15-19, NKJV)*

Jesus asked Peter, "Do you truly love me?" The Greek word here translated "love" is *agapao*. You have heard of *agape*, which is the purest and strongest form of love (the same word used to describe God's perfect love in John 3:16). Jesus asked Peter: "Do you love me, *with the purest and strongest form of love*, more than the rest?"

But Peter, now broken over his failures, couldn't bring himself to tell Jesus that he did. When Peter answered, He used the Greek word *phileo*, which doesn't have the same intensity as *agape*. Agape represents the pure and perfect love of God, whereas *phileo* represents brotherly love, friendship, and fondness of someone. It seems that Peter has been greatly humbled—and even embarrassed. He's discovered that he's got a long way to go and wasn't as strong and dedicated as he had thought he was. After Peter's total rejection of Jesus, it would have been perfectly right for Jesus to totally reject him. For this reason, Peter was *extremely* grateful that Jesus was still with him and willing to forgive and restore him.

Jesus, seeing Peter's humility, honored him by entrusting him with a new responsibility: "Feed my lambs."

The Greek word translated here as "feed" is the word *boskō,* which means "to provide for them pasture, a place to feed, to feed them and give them a place to graze." Jesus was honoring Peter's humility, saying, "Provide My sheep a pasture so they can eat and graze."

Jesus then asked the question again:

"Simon, son of Jonah, do you love (agapao) Me?"

Peter responded:

"Yes, Lord; You know that I love (phileo) You."

Jesus, seeing Peter's humility, once again responded by entrusting an even greater task to Peter:

"Tend My sheep."

The word translated here as "tend my sheep" is the Greek word *poimano*, which means "to rule and lead a herd of sheep." This is the second and most honoring command that Jesus gave Peter during this restoration process. He was now saying to Peter: "I don't only want you to provide pasture for my sheep and feed them. I also want you to be their leader ... to guide and disciple them as they endeavor to follow me." At this point, perhaps Peter thought, "I couldn't even keep my *own* commitment to the Lord. So how then am I going to lead others?" Jesus was restoring Peter to the place he needed to be before Jesus returned to Heaven.

Level Ground

But in verse 17, Jesus came down to Peter's level.

> *"He said to him the third time, 'Simon, son of Jonah, do you love (phileo) Me?'"*

This time, instead of using the Greek word *agapao*, which He had used earlier, Jesus used the word *phileo*. Why this change in language? I think Jesus was saying to Peter, "I know where you are right now, and I am meeting you right there. I am going to bring you to where you need to be because now I see a humble heart inside of you."

But:

> *"Peter was hurt because Jesus asked him the third time, 'Do you love Me?' He said, 'Lord, You know all things; You know that I love You.' Jesus said to him, 'Feed My sheep.'"* (John 21:17, NIV)

I want to clarify something that is very, *very* important as we look at these verses. There is a reason Jesus gave Peter the opportunity to verbally reaffirm his faith, his loyalty, and his love of Jesus as recorded in these passages.

After denying Jesus three times in the garden, Peter then denied Jesus three times in and around the courtyard. Then, in and around the courtyard, he not only denied Jesus three times verbally but denied him with an oath, calling down curses on himself. This was not something that was taken lightly in those days, and it is not something we should take lightly today. Jesus said in Matthew 12:37:

> *"For by thy words thou shalt be justified, and by thy words thou shalt be condemned."*

Jesus knew the power of words and was providing Peter the opportunity to remove the curse he had invoked on himself.

Jesus Focused On Peter
In this scene on the seashore, as Jesus appeared to the disciples, He focused His attention very directly on Peter. This was the same Peter He had spoken the following words to:

> *"Blessed art thou, Simon Barjona: for flesh and blood hath not revealed it unto thee, but my Father which is in heaven. And I say also unto thee, That thou art Peter [Petros – Stone], and upon this rock [Petra – Rock] I will build my church; and the gates of hell shall not prevail against it."* *(Matthew 16:17-18)*

Jesus was committed to Peter. He loved him and wanted to walk him through this restoration process word by word and line by line. He had no intention of throwing in the towel on this dear child of God. He had prophesied the plan of God over his life, and no matter how much Peter had messed up, Jesus knew he had come to his senses and was broken, humble, repentant, and ready for restoration and revival.

I am sure that Jesus, as He walked Peter through this divine process of restoration, looked right into Peter's eyes and deep into his heart. Jesus knew when someone was trying to deceive Him. He could spot a Pharisee from a mile away, blindfolded. Peter was real, and he was ready to make things right.

Before leaving for Heaven, Jesus wanted Peter to know that all was well. Peter's sins were forgiven. Jesus was restoring him into a right relationship with Him and into His rightful place in ministry. He knew Peter was going to be much more effective in ministry in his new humble condition than he had ever been before, when he was full of pride and spiritual arrogance. That's how God works! He looks on the heart, not on the outward appearance. He will find a way to break the things in us that He knows will eventually break us. Why? Because He loves us! He loves you, my friend—just as you are, but too much to leave you that way!

This divine appointment by the seashore came to an end with Jesus' speaking these words to His disciple Peter, letting him know some of what his future held. It wasn't all going to be pleasant. Persecution and many difficulties lay ahead, but Jesus left Peter with a command to follow Him.

*"I tell you the truth, when you were younger you dressed yourself and went where you wanted; but when you are old you will stretch out your hands, and someone else will dress and lead you where you do not want to go. Jesus said this to indicate the kind of death by which Peter would glorify God. Then He said, '**Follow me!**'" (John 21:18-19, NIV)*

How About Us?

- Are there weights of sin in your life that have easily been besetting you?
- Are you carrying weights of anger, discouragement, fear, false judgment, jealousy, envy, selfishness, or spiritual pride?
- Do you want to be freed of those today?
- Do you want to have the same kind of restoration Peter had—the kind that brings renewal and revival to your life like never before?

If so, let me assure you of something. If you will humble yourself and call on the name of the Lord, Jesus will meet you right where you are and give you the same kind of restoration that He gave Peter.

- He will forgive you.
- He will restore you.
- He will renew you.
- He will revive you.
- Then He will send you out as an ambassador to represent Him because then you will be ready to represent Jesus in the way He wants to be represented, not in a distorted, prideful, and negatively religious way.

We are all at different places in our love relationship with Jesus and our Heavenly Father, but God wants to bring restoration to each of us. He may ask me:

"Brian, do you really love Me more than these? I see you were judging with false judgment. Brian, do you really love Me?"

How will we respond? I think we should respond in this way:

"Yes Lord, I love You ... but not totally the way I want to."

Then, perhaps He would say to us:

"You can lead My sheep."

WHAT NOW?

Slide forward into the Great Commission

I hope this book has been both a challenge and a blessing to you. I wouldn't doubt that God has used it to bring you into a restored relationship with Him. Peter's story is very powerful, and it really relates to many of our lives. It certainly relates to mine.

I am convinced that one of the worst ways we have backslidden from the heart of God is that we have neglected His call to world missions and to worldwide evangelism. If we are walking in revival, the natural outflow of that revived relationship with the Lord is to sacrifice all we can to get His message to the whole world, not just to those in our "Jerusalem."

Before Jesus ascended into Heaven, He left one main command for His disciples: "Go into all the world and preach the Gospel to every creature." To deny caring for the lost and the hurting is to deny Jesus in a very significant way.

Many choose selfishness in the midst of a starving, hurting, and lost world. It is as if in our hearts we are saying to God, "I am not interested in what You want me to do." This is a sad place to be and a *sure sign* of a backslidden heart. We need to live each day seeking to fulfill our part of the Great Commission.

What is the Great Commission?

God's Great Commission is described in the Gospels and in the Book of Acts. Jesus has already done the work necessary for salvation. Oswald J. Smith reaffirmed that the "only task Jesus left us to do is the evangelization of the world." He asked, "Are we doing it?" But what is the Great Commission, according to the Word of God? These verses make it clear:

- "Go therefore and make disciples of all the nations, baptizing them, and teaching them to do all that I have commanded you to do." (Matthew 28:19)
- "And this gospel of the kingdom will be preached in the whole world as a testimony to all nations, and then the end will come." (Matthew 24:14)
- "He told them, 'The harvest is plentiful, but the workers are few. Ask the Lord of the harvest, therefore, to send out workers into his harvest field.'" (Luke 10:2)
- "Go into all the world and preach the gospel to all creation." (Mark 16:15)

Realize that the Great Commission is a call to reach the whole world with the Gospel. Jesus asks us to "make disciples of all nations" (Matthew 28:19), to preach the Gospel "in the whole world" (Matthew 24:14), and to preach the Gospel to "all creation" (Mark 16:15). In other words, if there is a place on the face of the earth, God wants the Gospel to go there. God wants every single creature and people group to have the opportunity to hear and respond to the Gospel. The book of Revelation says that people from every tribe and tongue will be in Heaven (Revelation 7:9). In other words, God is not closing the book of history until at least one person from each of the 16,750 people groups on the earth has heard and responded to the gospel.

If our task is to reach every people group with the gospel, how many people groups are there left for us to reach? An unreached people group is a group whose population consists of 5% or less professing Christians (of any tradition), mostly due to a lack of missions effort.

In order to assess how much still must be done to fulfill this Great Commission, we have to look at what has been done and what remains to be done. Good statistics can help us do that. Leonard Ravenhill once said:

"To be spiritually minded is joy and peace, but to be statistically minded can be very disturbing."

Are All Nations Reached?
Are there really that many people who have never heard the Gospel, in this age of radio, television, and Internet? The sad answer is yes. I have been to their countries and seen their faces. 6,921 people groups, making up 40.6 percent of the world's population, are still unreached with the Gospel. Friends, that is 2.84 billion people who are going to slip into a helpless eternity without Jesus unless someone preaches to them.

The majority of unreached people groups live in an area of the world called the "10/40 Window." As a matter of fact, 85% of these unreached people groups reside there. The 10/40 Window is an area between the coordinates of 10 degrees longitude and 40 degrees latitude, and a very large part of the world's population lives there, trapped in spiritual darkness.

It seems as though it would be a "no brainer" for Christians to sacrifice their money and some comforts of this life to reach these dear lost, dying souls. They are on a beeline to hell. Who will do it? Will you?

If you are not going to preach to them, then you must send a substitute. The worst thing that you can do is … nothing. If you do nothing, then you are choosing to be a part of the problem.

What We Could Do – Reach the Unreached

The task of reaching the unreached is great and difficult but *not* impossible. In fact, if every professing evangelical Christian would give *something* towards this cause, then we could immediately begin to bring the Gospel to these Gospel-starved countries. Consider these statistics from The Traveling Team:

- "Evangelical Christians could provide all of the funds needed to plant a church in each of the 6,900 unreached people groups with only 0.03% of their income.
- The Church has roughly 3,000 times the financial resources and 9,000 times the manpower needed to finish the Great Commission.
- If every evangelical gave 10% of their income to missions we could easily support 2 million new missionaries."

Do you see what potential we have to bring the Gospel to the world if only we would all just sacrifice a little? Sadly, we are not living up to our world missions potential *at all*. We are putting our money in *the wrong places*.

Pampering the Pampered

Consider this: 85% of all American tithes and offerings go towards *running the show*. That means that 50% of American tithes go to paying staff and pastors, 20% pays for the upkeep and expansion of buildings, and 15% pays for church expenses such as electricity and supplies (*The Traveling Team*). How strange this must be to God. Every day, He is forced to look at our waste against the backdrop of a world starving for food and the Gospel. We are pampering the pampered instead of reaching the unreached. This shows how we have backslidden in heart.

Reaching the Reached

Did you know that only 15% of American tithes and offerings go towards outreach of any kind? That's right: 15%! Wouldn't you at least hope that a good amount of that 15% would be dedicated to reaching those who have never been reached with the Gospel? But of the 15% of offerings spent on outreach, only 0.5% goes to reach unreached people groups. 1.5% goes towards foreign nations that have already been reached with the Gospel, and the remaining 13% goes to reaching America. Every year, an enormous $26,970,000,000 is spent to reach the foreign reached world. That's 87% of the money given to "missions." Every year, a comparatively tiny $310,000,000 is spent to reach the unreached world. That's only 1% of the money given to "missions"! (The Traveling Team)

Here I want to share an excerpt from a book by Oswald J. Smith originally titled *Passion for Souls*. In this excerpt he shares an illustration about the importance of reaching the whole world and everyone in it with the Gospel.

"Do you remember when the Lord Jesus Christ fed the five thousand? Do you recall how He had them sit down, row upon row, on the green grass? Then do you remember how He took the loaves and fishes and blessed them and then broke them and gave them to His disciples? And do you remember how the disciples started at one end of the front row and went right along that front row giving everyone a helping? Then do you recall how they turned right around and started back along that front row again, asking everyone to take a second helping? Do you remember?

"No? A thousand times no! Had they done that, those in the back rows would have been rising up and protesting most vigorously. 'Here,' they would have been saying, 'Come back here. Give us a helping. We have not had any yet. We are starving; it isn't right; it isn't fair. Why should those people in the front rows have a second helping before we have had a first?'

"And they would have been right. We talk about the second blessing. They haven't had the first blessing yet. We talk about the second coming of Christ. They haven't heard about the first coming yet. It just isn't fair. 'Why should anyone hear the Gospel twice before everyone has heard it once?' You know as well as I do, that not one individual in that entire company of five thousand men, besides women and children, got a second helping until everyone had a first helping.

"I have never known a minister to have any trouble with the back rows. All his trouble comes from the front rows. Those in the front rows are over-fed, and they develop spir-

itual indigestion. They tell him how much to feed them; when to feed them; when to stop feeding them; how long to feed them; what kind of food to give them, etc. etc., and if he doesn't do it, they complain and find fault. If a minister had any sense, he would leave the front rows for a while and let them get hungry for once in their lives and go to the back rows, and then when he returned they would be ready to accept his ministry, and there would be no murmuring or complaining.

"My friends, I have been with the back rows. I have seen the countless millions in those back rows famishing for the Bread of Life. Is it right? Should we be concentrating on the front rows? Ought we not rather to be training the front rows to share what they have with the back rows, and thus reach them with the Gospel, those for whom nothing has been prepared?"

This is certainly a sign of a backslidden heart and of a backslidden church. None of us can control what church leaders do with the money they have been entrusted with, but we as individuals need to be a lot wiser with our offerings. We need to put faithfulness to the call of God first and let everything else take the 100th place on our list of important things to do. Do you remember the seven churches in Revelation chapters 2 and 3? Of all of the churches, only the church at Philadelphia was totally on track with God's plan. We must be like the believers in that church. We must not partake in the Laodicean legacy. Friends, leave that legacy to all of the others who are content to compromise. They are living for things that won't amount to much of anything in the Kingdom of Heaven, but don't let them drag you down with them.

As you can see, there is so much more we can do. In so many respects we are falling short of the goal. Every day, people slip into eternity without Jesus—Jesus who died to save sinners, including you and me. It is wrong. It is sinful for us to sit idly by, doing little to nothing, when the power to do so much good is at our fingertips.

When this life is over, and we inhabit eternity, we will certainly all have some regrets over how we spent our time and efforts and resources in this life. But we can ease those regrets by choosing *right now* to focus on the things that really matter to God. Let's join together and focus on giving as God would have us give, on caring as God would have us care, and on living as God would have us live.

Let Us Pray

"Father God, You know my heart, You see where I am strong, and You see where I am weak. You see where I am prideful, and You see where I am humble. God, my desire is for You to do whatever needs to be done in my life to bring me to that place of total surrender to You. Father, I want to jump on the potter's wheel, knowing that You are the Potter and I am the clay. I trust You with my whole life, my spirit, my mind, my will, my emotions, and my body. I entrust all these to You!

"God, I know that if you bring me into a trial, it is to build strength inside of me. Would You show me today, by the power of the Holy Spirit, where I am in my relationship

with You? Have I been denying You relationally? Have I been denying You publicly? I am ready for Repentance, Restoration, Renewal, and Revival in my life! God, I know Your call is for me to know You and to make You known. So, today, I want to say to You, 'here I am, send me.' Please equip me, purify me, and peel the scales from my eyes so that I can see this life the way You do. I want to see lost and hurting people the way You do and go as Your ambassador to give the message of hope and salvation that is found in Your Son, Jesus."

AN ENCOURAGING NOTE

I want to encourage you to remember that as a disciple of Jesus you are in full-time ministry. You are a *full-time minister* of the Gospel! That is an exciting calling, and a calling that comes with a responsibility. We are each individually responsible to fulfill His call on our lives.

I always say that two of the greatest abilities we can have are *avail*-ability and *response*-ability. *Availability* is being available to hear the call of God. Availability is demonstrated in saying, "Here I am, Lord, send me." *Responsibility* is the ability to respond to God's call once we have heard it and then to fulfill it in our lives. Many people hear the call of God to do a task of some type but quit before it is done. They grow tired and give up because of lack of faith or discouragement. This is what Jesus said about His call:

> *"'My food,' said Jesus, 'is to do the will of him who sent me and to finish his work.'" (John 4:34, NIV)*

We must be willing to finish the work we start, just as God is willing to finish the work He has started in us.

"Being confident of this, that he who began a good work in you will carry it on to completion until the day of Christ Jesus." (Philippians 1:6, NIV)

Please remember that God has strategically placed you in society as an Ambassador of Jesus Christ. He has placed you in a specific family, school and/or job, neighborhood, city, state, and country. That is where He wants you to shine, and then beyond that spot He wants to use you through world missions by either going or sending.

If you are actively taking those opportunities that God is placing before you, I want to commend you. I also want to warn you because the enemy of your soul will do everything he can to distract you and turn you away from those divine appointments God places in your life. Another tactic he uses when you respond within the divine appointments is to do everything he can to get you to speak out of your own heart instead of under the divine unction and direction of the Holy Spirit. He wants you to misrepresent God and to say "religious" things that sound good but are not what Jesus wants to say in those situations. He is counting on us to know His voice and to speak His words.

Or maybe you are the person who says, "I am just too shy—I can't do that." I want to encourage you to break through the fear! God knows, I was one of the shyest people you could ever meet when I first came to the Lord. God changed all that. The Holy Spirit saw the desire in my heart to be faithful to Him and saw my attempts at walking by faith and lifted me up by His power and might. The love God has placed in believers' hearts longs to come out! God pours it into us to bless us but also so He can pour it *out* of us. He wants to pour it out on the hungry, searching souls around us.

I will leave you with something the Lord spoke to my heart back in 1975 when I was just 19 years old. It happened one night when I had driven to a destination the Lord put on my heart to go to so I could witness about Jesus to people on the streets. I was sitting in my 1963 Ford Fairlane 500 trying to muster up enough courage to get out of my car and start doing what I was there to do. What I heard that night was not an audible voice, but it was loud enough for me to hear and to remember that experience all these years. The Holy Spirit said:

"Their need to hear is greater than your fear to share."

That was all I needed to hear! I stepped out of my car and have been sharing the Gospel ever since.

May God bless you as you move forward in your walk with the Lord. Remind yourself every day that God loves you and has called you and embark on a new adventure with Him every day until He returns!

—Brian Weller

For more from Brian Mark Weller,
or to learn more about Message
Ministries & Missions Inc.,
please visit:

WWW.BRIANMARKWELLER.COM
WWW.MESSAGEMINISTRIES.ORG

www.ingramcontent.com/pod-product-compliance
Lightning Source LLC
Chambersburg PA
CBHW060611030426
42337CB00018B/3039